Thick Fog

by Frederick James
illustrated by George Ulrich

Practice Decodable 35

McGraw Hill Education

Bothell, WA • Chicago, IL • Columbus, OH • New York, NY

MHEonline.com

Send all inquiries to:
McGraw-Hill Education
8787 Orion Place
Columbus, OH 43240

ISBN: 978-0-02-145359-7
MHID: 0-02-145359-4

Printed in China

8 9 10 11 12 DSS 27 26 25 24 23

There was thick fog.

Beth had a big truck on a path.

This truck had shrimp.
Can Beth see in thick fog?

Beth did not see Gramps's Shrimp Shop.
Then a flash hit the shop.

Flash! Flash! Flash! Flash!

On the fifth flash, Beth spotted it.

Josh had flashed.

"I helped that truck," he said.